Musée d'Orsay
Spirit of place

by Caroline Mathieu

nouvelles éditions
scaLa

The origins of Orsay

Located right in the heart of Paris on the left bank of the Seine, across the river from the Tuileries gardens and not far from the Louvre, the Musée d'Orsay has the advantage of an outstanding site, an unusual building – a railway station transformed into a museum – and collections that are exceptional in their range and quality.

The location has experienced times of glory and times of tragedy; at the beginning of the 17th century it was still countryside, and the famous Tour de Nesles – which stood on the site of the Institut – marked the western boundary of Paris. This whole district was a meeting place favoured by duellists and ruffians, an atmosphere of the kind described by Victor Hugo! Margaret of Valois, commonly known as "la Reine Margot", the wife repudiated by

∧ Aerial view showing the position of the station across the river from the Tuileries gardens and the Louvre.

< View taken from the roof of the Musée d'Orsay.

Henri IV, took up residence here in 1606, establishing an estate covering 16 hectares along the river as a setting for her mansion. When she died in 1615 deep in debt, her property was broken up and sold by lots; the streets familiar to us today were once the paths through the park: the rue du Bac, the rue de Bellechasse and the rue de Poitiers, while the rue de Lille (formerly known as the rue de Bourbon) was the main avenue.

In the 18th century the district which until then had been wasteland with a few scattered dwelling houses became one of the prime residential areas of the Parisian aristocracy, housing splendid private mansions, including the Hôtel de Salm, now the museum of the Legion of Honour, which was built between 1782 and 1788. However, the river port known as La Grenouillère, used for storing wood rafted down the Seine, was still in existence. In 1708 the risk of fire led Charles Boucher d'Orsay, the provost of the merchants of Paris, to construct the quai or embankment that bears his name; it was completed during the Empire.

> Extract from the plan by Turgot: La Grenouillère and the rafted wood between the rue de Bourbon (rue de Lille) and the embankment.

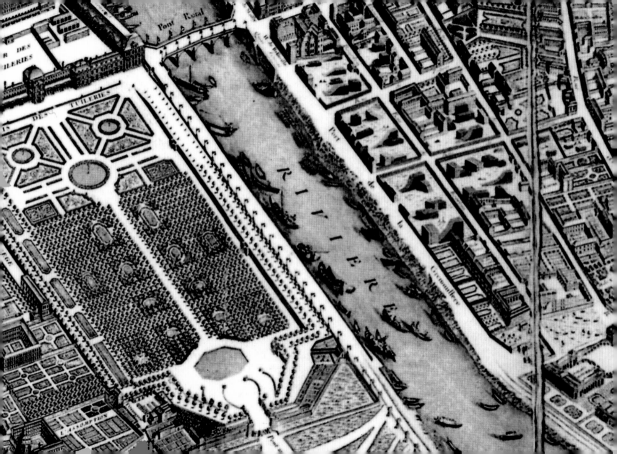

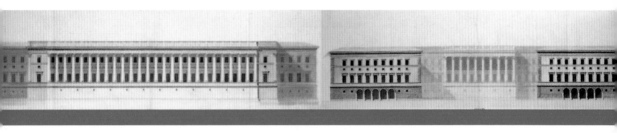

The Palais of Orsay

The second major development came in 1810 when Napoleon I decided on the construction of a building intended for the Ministry of Foreign Affairs. This new palace was to be the symbol of the influence of France radiating out across Europe and the world.

The scheme was entrusted to Jacques Charles Bonnard (1765-1818), but work had scarcely started when the architect died, and it was broken off in 1820. The building was then assigned to the Auditor General's Office and the Council of State. Work on the palace was resumed by Jacques Lacornée, and it was completed in 1838 in the reign of Louis-Philippe. The large building along the lines of a Roman palazzo with architecture that was imposing but not very practical was embellished by decorations that were entrusted to celebrated painters, including Théodore Chassériau (1819-1856), who carried out his finest decorative scheme in the staircase, devoted to three allegories: *Peace, War* and *Trade*.

∧ Jacques-Charles Bonnard, Ministry of Foreign Affairs, 1808, elevations of the façades overlooking the Seine and the rue de Lille.

< The Palais of Orsay.

∧ Ruins of Paris: panorama of the monuments destroyed by fire from the quai d'Orsay.

The fire

On 24 May 1871, at the height of the bloody events associated with the Commune, a fire devastated the Palais d'Orsay. Appreciable remnants of Chassériau's compositions were subsequently rescued from the charred walls; they have now been restored and are held at the Louvre. During that terrible week in May

City of Paris, the Tuileries Palace and part of the new Louvre built by Hector Lefuel were completely burnt down. The Hôtel de Ville and the Hôtel de Salm were rebuilt, whereas the ruins of the Tuileries remained as they were until 1882 and those of the Palais d'Orsay were left for thirty years, tangible evidence of that tragic episode in the history of Paris.

All extant fragments of the decorative work – sculptures by Clésinger, columns, handrails, grilles, balconies and candelabra – were sold at auction in 1898.

much of the Deposit and Consignment Office and the Hôtel de Salm (now the museum of the Legion of Honour) was destroyed, while the Hôtel de Ville with all the archives of the

< The ruins of Paris — grand
staircase, Cour des
Comptes.

Antique ruins

While people were considering the fate of the ruins, the skeleton of the palace played host to an extraordinary wild garden in which pollens from exotic plants cultivated in nearby greenhouses developed, and botanists came to study them. The site, which was teeming with vegetation and mosses, became a destination for outings and aroused the astonishment of one of the reporters from *La Revue Illustrée* in 1888: "Once we had reached the burnt palace that used to house the Cour des Comptes, my friend stopped in delight. He admired the amazing vegetation that had

developed there in less than seventeen years: brambles obstructing the apertures, mosses coating the pilasters, coarse grass growing in the cracks; an improvised virgin forest the roots of which lift the paving stones, dislodge the steps on the flights of stairs, and make this relatively new pile of rubble look like the most beautiful antique ruins."

Of course the idea of restoring the palace and returning it to its original purpose was considered, but the project would have been far too dear; there was also a notion that the building might be devoted to the future Museum of Decorative Arts, and with that in mind Auguste

Rodin received the commission for the *Porte de l'Enfer* (Gates of Hell) in 1880. Through the ups and downs of history, the original plaster version of that work was to return to the place for which it had been designed, as it is now held in the Musée d'Orsay's collections.

∧ **Edmond Allouard,**
The Ruins of Cour des Comptes, circa 1895.

CHEMIN DE FER D'ORLÉANS
GARE DU QUAI D'ORSAY-HÔTEL TERMINUS.
- AVANT- PROJET -

The gare d'Orsay

In anticipation of the 1900 Exposition universelle and in response to an application submitted by the Orleans Railway Company pointing out how far its terminus at Austerlitz was from the centre, the idea of constructing a central station was considered. This proposal aroused very lively fears that one of the finest sites in Paris would be permanently disfigured by a dirty, noisy building with an industrial appearance. The Company managed to buy the plot and, to placate all these criticisms, turned to three highly regarded architects, Emile Bénard (1844-1929), Victor Laloux (1850-1937) and Lucien Magne (1849-1916), asking them to give thought to the general layout and the architectural character of the building, in the three following eventualities: a scheme for a station without a hotel, a scheme for a station with a subsidiary hotel, and a scheme for a station with a major hotel on the corner of the river embankment and the rue de Bellechasse.

∧ Émile Bénard, design of the façade for a "station with a major hotel".

< Émile Bénard, interior perspective.

< Scheme by Victor
  Laloux: "station
  with a major hotel",
  for the competition
  for Orsay, 1898.

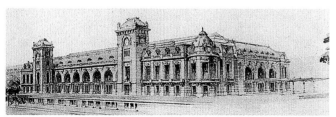

The competition

The nearness of the Louvre, the Tuileries and the Hôtel de Salm ruled out the possibility of constructing a building with a visible metallic framework, still considered too utilitarian for the heart of historic Paris. Magne suggested façades treated as arcaded galleries linked by corner pylons; Bénard put the emphasis on the central concourse, formed by iron groin vaults, and in a second project gave the façade overlooking the embankment a stone tower with a clock and a belvedere at the top, in

> Victor Laloux
in his studio.

order to introduce "a touch of the unexpected and picturesque on this bank of the Seine", as he said!

It was the scheme by Victor Laloux that was selected on 21 April 1898. Laloux had been awarded the Major Rome Prize in 1878 and was a professor of architecture at the École des Beaux-Arts; he designed many buildings in Tours, his native town (the Basilica of St Martin, the Hôtel de Ville, the station...). In 1908 he was involved in building the Crédit Lyonnais. He designed a monumental all-stone station, with a 370-bedroom hotel attached to it. The station consisted of a porch opening onto the embankment, a vestibule where all the departure services were located and a large 40-metre wide concourse forming just a single aisle, with two naves of unequal height. The long façade along the embankment was composed of seven arcades framed by two pavilions with clocks, and the terrace was punctuated by three statues.

> Overleaf: Victor Laloux:
Gare d'Orsay, scheme for
the façade overlooking
the embankment.

< Two schemes
by Lucien Magne
for a "station without
a hotel", competition
for Orsay, 1898.

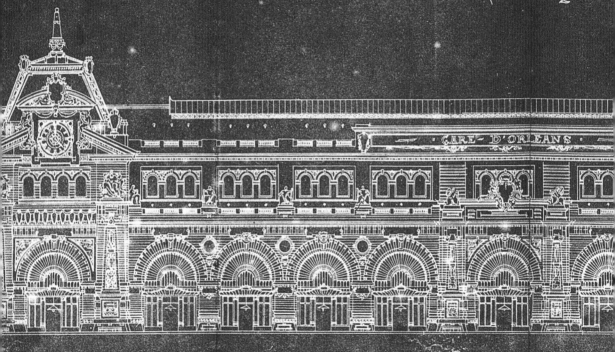

GARE DU QUAI

GARE D'ORLEANS

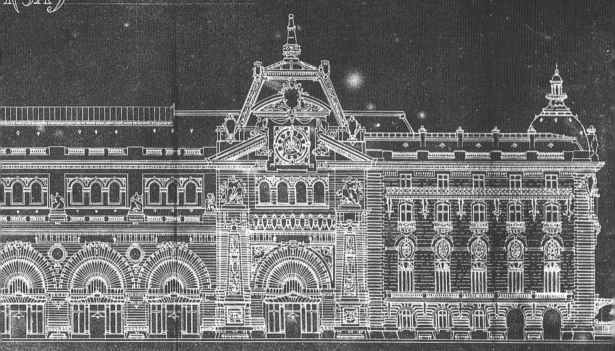

> 1 October 1899: building site for the Gare d'Orsay.

The building site

The demolition of the Palais d'Orsay was started in April 1898 and completed on 4 August. Work progressed quickly in spite of the difficulties caused by frequent flooding; the foundations were completed in May 1899, and the entire building was officially opened in July 1900. A double underground tunnel allowed direct communication with the bank of the Seine where materials were delivered; 3,650 metres of track, above and below ground, had to be built to link up with Austerlitz, the metal frame of the station had to be put up, and then the stone that would clad it was bonded to it: white limestone from quarries at Souppes (Seine-et-Marne), Vilhonneur (Charente) and Chauvigny (Vienne).

Shifts of 300 workmen by day and 80 by night on a well-lit building site allowed the work to be completed in two years. And yet a great many problems had to be resolved, first and foremost the roofing of the great 40-metre concourse which supported all the plasterwork decoration. Furthermore the structural frame of the concourse was

integral with that of the domed vestibules along the embankment, and both rested on the same supports.

The technology of building in metal had been perfectly mastered since the construction of the extraordinary "gallery of machines" for the 1889 Exposition universelle. But everything was concealed behind stone, and the large metal gable topped by the head of Mercury, the god of travellers, was masked on the rue de Bellechasse side by the façade of the hotel, which had a large iron and glass canopy in front of it.

L'inauguration

"The station is superb and looks like an art gallery," wrote the painter Édouard Detaille. The station started operating in May 1900, and was officially opened on 14 July; it was the first modern station designed for electric traction: at Austerlitz, steam engines were exchanged for electric ones, which explains the luxurious appearance of the concourse, the roof of which was decorated with floral motifs made of sculpted and painted plaster, so that it resembled the great baths or basilicas of the Imperial Roman period. All the services were located in dome-covered vestibules on the ground floor; sloping ramps and goods lifts had been designed for the luggage, lifts for the travellers, and the platforms were at the same height as the carriages, so avoiding the need for steps; there were fifteen tracks beneath the embankment and the Deposit Office.

< The hotel and the station decked with flags, thirteen days before the official opening.

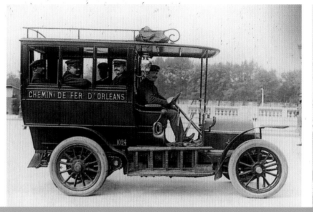

∧ The Orleans Railway
Shuttle bus.

> The rail tracks below
ground, with an electric
engine in the foreground.

The main station concourse was 138 metres long by 40 metres wide and 32 metres high; the whole metal structure was concealed by stone cladding that enclosed a hotel with 370 bedrooms, almost all provided with bathrooms, a level of comfort that was unusual for the period. It extended in five superimposed storeys overlooking the rue de Lille, the rue de Bellechasse and a small part of the embankment; particular care had been devoted to the decoration of the banqueting room and the restaurant.

Victor Laloux had designed all the detail of the ornamentation with splendid eclecticism, associating Louis XIV, Louis XV and Louis XVI styles. He had entrusted the decoration to

officially recognized artists: the paintings in the departure hall were by Fernand Cormon, those in the restaurant by Gabriel Ferrier (*Allegory of the periods of time*) and Benjamin Constant (*The roads of the air*), and those in the banqueting room by Pierre Fritel (*The chariot of Apollo*). Three large sculptures, symbolising the cities of Toulouse (by Laurent Marqueste), Bordeaux (by Jean-Baptiste Hugues) and Nantes (by Jean-Antoine Injalbert who endowed the sculpture with Madame Laloux's features) provided accents on the façade overlooking the Seine..

∧ The restaurant
  of the Orsay hotel.

< The departure hall.

The flood

In January 1910, heavy rain following heavy snowfalls gave rise to the worst flooding that century! In the course of a few days the Seine rose 8.5 metres above its normal level; whole districts were under water, and torrents of water sped along the rue du Bac, the rue de Poitiers and the rue de Bellechasse. The underground track between Austerlitz and Orsay was soon affected, traffic was halted and the electricity supply disrupted. The Gare d'Orsay, under more than 5 metres of water, was nicknamed the "Gare d'Ys", Ys being the name of a legendary Breton city believed to have been submerged in the 4th or 5th century. People came to catch a few large fish and look at their reflected image floating in the water...

The metamorphoses of Orsay

Over forty years the Gare d'Orsay, as the Paris terminus for the south-west of France, witnessed the departure of nearly 200 trains a day. But progress in electrification and mechanisation made the station difficult to run; the number of carriages increased, making the trains much longer so that the platforms were too short. As early as 1929, SNCF (French Railways) planned to give it up, and in 1935 they suggested doing it up in the modern style and turning it into a palace for festivals and sports. Finally on 23 November 1939 main-line traffic was halted once and for all, and only the service running to the Paris suburbs remained: the most modern station of its day was transformed into a great empty, abandoned shell...

Laloux's monument then became the scene of the most varied events and activities: a centre for dispatching parcels to prisoners of war, a reception centre for prisoners and deportees. In May 1958 General de Gaulle chose to hold a press conference announcing his return to politics and his policy in the banqueting room of the hotel, which was to close its doors in January 1973.

∧ General de Gaulle's press conference in May 1958.

< All the faces of Orsay: 1945, reception centre for prisoners of war.

∧ Michael Lonsdale and
Anthony Perkins during
the shooting of *The Trial*
by Orson Welles.

Treading the boards

With its "Piranesian" aspect as a vast space inhabited only by air and light, the main concourse inspired film directors: in 1962 Orson Welles filmed The Trial based on Kafka there, and in 1970 Bernardo Bertolucci shot various scenes for The Conformist.

Over a longer period, from November 1973 to April 1980, the theatre company of Jean-Louis Barrault and Madeleine Renaud set up shop at the back of the large nave, bringing back life to the great desert of iron and glass, before moving on to the Théâtre du Rond-Point on the Champs-Élysées. In January 1974, while waiting for the new Hôtel Drouot to be built, the Company of Registered Auctioneers took up temporary residence there until May 1980. Then a new life could begin for Orsay!

∧ Drouot salerooms on the left bank.

< Jean-Louis Barrault.

∧ Model of scheme
by Jean Faugeron.

> Scheme by Le Corbusier,
façade.

A luxury hotel

It took a fight to save Orsay! From the 1960s on there was talk of demolishing it: "Nobody will shed tears for the Laloux building; although completed in 1900, it possesses none of the graces of that period and houses a mediocre metal frame behind its stone façades, which are unparalleled in Paris for their heaviness."

SNCF considered building a luxury hotel with between 1,000 and 1,500 bedrooms. Le Corbusier, among others, came up with plans, elevations and models; a first prize was even awarded to the scheme by the architects Coulon and Gillet. It ultimately took a crime against architecture, the destruction of the market halls by Baltard in 1972, to save the station.

∧ Le Corbusier : entrance hall of the hotel
and terrace of the restaurant 8 metres above
the embankment.

au niveau 4
Hall de l'Hôtel
et terrasse du restaurant
à 8 mètres
au dessus du quai
de la Seine

$\frac{27}{\overline{I}}$
61   le Corbusier

A new scheme for Orsay

In 1970, permission to demolish the station was granted, but Jacques Duhamel, the Minister for Cultural Affairs under President Georges Pompidou, ruled against the building of the hotel designed by the architects Coulon and Gillet. In 1973 the station was put on the supplementary list of Historic Monuments, then in 1978 it was listed. The Directorate of the Museums of France then suggested using it to set up a museum intended to display all forms of artistic expression dating from the second half of the 19th century and the early years of the 20th, thus establishing a connecting link between the Louvre and the collections of the Georges Pompidou Centre and making it possible to express their full richness. The scheme was accepted by Georges Pompidou and was later supported by Valéry Giscard d'Estaing and François Mitterand. A programming study was commissioned in 1974; an analysis of the buildings had to be made and the possibility of implanting a museum in them had to be studied. In 1978 the State organised a competition with three leading architects at the

∧ Presenting the models to M. Valéry Giscard d'Estaing, the President of the Republic.

∧ From left to right:
Pierre Colboc,
Renaud Bardon
and Jean-Paul Philippon.

> Perspective section of the
raised pavement and the
rue de Lille gallery (design
by ACT Architecture).

Historic Monuments department, two leading architects working on civilian buildings and national palaces, and a team of three young architects working in partnership, ACT Architecture, as the contenders. The scheme by ACT was selected.

ACT

It was a team of three architects, Pierre Colboc, Renaud Bardon and Jean-Paul Philippon, who emerged victorious from the consultation process. They proposed making the main entrance to the museum on the rue de Bellechasse, organising the exhibits along the large nave by opening it out so as to preserve the vastness of the space, and building on either side of a large central aisle, using the domed halls of the former station. At the top, the attic area almost lost in the sky was arranged to form a long gallery. The hotel reception rooms were integrated into the circuit. Laloux's metal pillars and girders and his stucco decorations were respected, restored and set off throughout, with the new structures leaving the existence of the original building very apparent.

Gae Aulendi

The forms of the interior architecture also had to be specified, the materials and colours chosen, the museum furniture designed and the installation of the collections thought out. Consultations for this purpose were started in March 1980 and in July 1981 the Italian architect Gae Aulenti was entrusted with the "mission of designing the internal arrangement, the decoration and the furniture and fittings of the museum". She proposed a powerful architecture, able to stand up to the immense volume of the nave, and elected to harmonise the rooms, all of them different, through the use for the floors and walls of Buxy stone, a flashed limestone from Burgundy. Gae Aulenti opted for clarity throughout, deciding to emphasise the original architecture and making rigorous but subtle use of the language of polychromy. Green – for the metal structures – and yellow – for the plasterwork coffering – were reserved for the original architectural materials used by Laloux, while the pink of the Buxy stone and the range of painted wall coverings – blue, orange and brown – went with the contemporary architecture.

∧ 1 December 1986,
President François
Mitterrand and Gae
Aulenti at the official
opening of the museum.

The building site

While the station had been built in two years, it took almost ten to design the museum, then carry out the work. Moreover, is it not paradoxical that a place dedicated to movement and noise should have been turned into a museum, a place of silence and intimacy conducive to the appreciation of works of art?

As early as 1980 work started on dismantling the Renaud-Barrault theatre and the floors that had been made to accommodate the auctioneers'salerooms. A great many technical problems had to be resolved: it was necessary to ensure weather-tightness, eliminate the vibrations caused by the running of the RER, install air-conditioning throughout the large volume, successfully absorb sounds and noises, light the exhibits harmoniously,

repair all the structures of the building and restore it to its original freshness. An active restoration policy again endowed the large nave with the luxurious appearance that Laloux had given it, making it possible to recover the colours and brilliance of the banqueting room and the restaurant.

The rose motifs in the nave were remade identically, and apart from their decorative appearance they perform two important functions: absorbing sounds thanks to the resonators placed at each corner, while an outlet grille placed at the centre provides one of the flow routes for the air conditioning. The system of bonding which is special to the museum, a line of holes dug out of the walls, also serves to absorb noises and prevent cacophony and confusion.

∧ View of the domed rooms, with the plasterwork rose-windows remade identically.

Dance by Carpeaux

Cleared of all builders' rubble, the museum stood clean and empty ready to receive the exhibits in July 1986. It took no less than six months to install the 2,000 or so paintings, 600 sculptures, architectural models, and the rooms of objets d'art, drawings and photographs. Seeing these works arriving and being installed was a period of intense emotion after years of working on models and photographs! In September, the transport of the Dance group by Carpeaux from the rooms at the Louvre to the Musée d'Orsay constituted a spectacular and sometimes worrying event. This group weighing 18 tonnes, made up of three parts, had been commissioned from the artist in 1863 by the architect Charles Garnier for his new opera house. As it was being eroded by Paris

pollution, it went to the Louvre in 1964 and a copy by Paul Belmondo took its place at the Opéra. The group had to be brought in before the pavilion above it dedicated to architecture and the decorative arts could be fitted up, and of course a specialist firm had to be employed. Then restorers came in to remake the joints, and tidy up and clean the stone.

The forecourt

The forecourt in front of the museum was fitted out after the whole building had been restored and cleaned and the collections installed. November 1986 saw the arrival on lorries with reinforced platforms of the Elephant by Fremiet, the Rhinoceros by Jacquemart and the Horse by Rouillard, which then performed an aerial ballet before being placed on their plinths! Like the figures of the Continents, these hollow-cast sculptures used to adorn the former Palais du Trocadéro, built for the 1878 Exposition universelle by the architect Gabriel Davioud and the engineer Jules Bourdais and demolished in 1936 to make way for the Palais de Chaillot, erected for yet another Exposition universelle, that held in 1937.

These groups had gone through a variety of adventures; the animals had finally been placed at the roundabout at the Porte de Saint-Cloud; Europe by Schoenewerk, Asia by Falguière, North America by Hiolle, South America by Aimé Millet, Africa by Delaplanche and Oceania by Mathurin Moreau had been abandoned and even left at a tip...

The musée d'Orsay

Inaugurated on 1 December 1986, the museum was exposed to widespread and harsh criticism. It was not only the museography and the architectural approach, but also the scientific choices, that were the object of controversy. The museum was reproached for having rehabilitated the "pompiers" (firemen), a term that discredited an era of painting that was very diverse, of which several players have since been rediscovered, and for not having given their due to the "artists of modernity", in other words the Impressionists, according to this facile over-simplification which almost sounded the death knell of the Gare...

Twenty-five years after its opening, the *musée d'Orsay* has experienced a major renovation. On the top floor, the Impressionist paintings are now exhibited in galleries entirely

∧ The entrance to the museum with its iron and glass awning.

< The Musée d'Orsay seen from the Quai des Tuileries.

redesigned by Jean-Michel Wilmotte, and the adjoining Amont pavilion has been radically transformed by Dominique Brard and the *Atelier de l'Île*, with the creation of four floors showcasing foreign decorative arts from before 1920. New temporary exhibition rooms have been created in what used to be the post-Impressionists gallery, and these works have been moved to the first level (Van Gogh, Gauguin, Seurat, Signac, and *les Nabis*) dialoguing with the sculptures on the terraces. Contemporary design is omnipresent, with the colourful, bright café on level 5, designed by the Brazilian brothers Humberto and Fernando Campana, and the glass benches created by Tokujin Yoshioka, which seem to be made of ice.

The central aisle

The aim of the museum, up to now with no equivalent in the world, is to assemble the whole of the artistic expressions from a very short, but fecund, period: 1848-1914. Here one can understand the links that exist between painting, sculpture, decorative arts and architecture, and photography. The museum's itinerary is arranged over three main levels, chronologically, in large sequences and by technique, and as often as possible by artist. The ground floor is devoted to the Second Empire; paintings are presented on each side of the central aisle allotted to them, while the terraces laid out on the first floor are devoted to sculpture which «turns» in the space and light. A series of landings leads to the two towers, at the feet of which is situated the "salle de l'Opéra", laid out by Richard Peduzzi and revealing the inventive eclecticism of this period. Architecture, drawing, and photography from the museum's collections are exhibited in thematic shows. Large exhibitions benefit from separate spaces situated at the beginning of the itinerary, along the former platform.

> The central aisle with
a small-scale model
of Auguste Bartholdi's
Statue of Liberty,
commissioned by
the French government
in 1900.

The Painting Rooms

On the ground floor, you can discover creations by major artists of the 1850s, whose works are closely linked to the beginning of the century, such as Ingres, Delacroix, and Chassériau, the painter of historical scene, as well as mythology, and Second Empire decorative arts. Next comes the beginning of Realism, with Millet and Courbet; around Manet, the beginning of New Painting with the first works by Monet, Bazille, Renoir, and Degas, as well as the singular work of Toulouse-Lautrec, which

The Luxembourg rooms,
on the ground floor
of the central nave.

tracks beauty in sordidness. Symbolism, which emerged in reaction to the excessive focus on reality among the Realists, Naturalists, and Impressionists, is represented in the precious and languid figures of Gustave Moreau, Puvis de Chavannes's search for inner serenity, as well as in the creations by Odilon Redon and *les Nabis,* principally Maurice Denis, a journey that closes with Vuillard's extraordinary cycle of *Public Gardens.* This circuit resonates with the rooms on the next level, devoted to Van Gogh and Gauguin, the neo-Impressionists, and *les Nabis.*

The Galerie of Impressionists

At the top of the building, the attic floor of the station, stretching between the two clock pavilions, sees the Impressionist adventure unfold, with Monet, Renoir, Pissarro, Sisley, Berthe Morisot, Caillebotte. Degas remains independent, empassioned by the "artificial life" of the race tracks or the opera, Cézanne rejects the ephemeral.

The former column gallery has been radically transformed to create a new exhibition space.

The First Floor

On the first floor, Rodin, Maillol and Bourdelle reign on the terraces; in the three first domed rooms are presented the large canvases favoured by the more official, naturalist or symbolist painters. The furniture collections and the more precious French, Belgian, Spanish and Italian Art Nouveau creations occupy the last three rooms. A spectacular collection of foreign paintings (Hodler, Munch, Klimt) breathes a new attitude. Several very decorated rooms recall the splendour of the former hotel; a ballroom and reception rooms accommodate the decorative arts of the Second Empire and the Third Republic, while the hotel restaurant has become that of the museum. The itinerary ends with the Nabis (Bonnard, Vuillard, Maurice Denis, Roussel).

> The Gauguin room.

Rooms on the first
two levels
of the Amont pavilion.

The Amont pavilion

Visitors can access this area from the
sculpture terrace on level one, and from the
Impressionists gallery. This superb new area
houses a magnificent collection of British,
German, Scandinavian, and Viennese art
nouveau, as well as late French art nouveau.
These rooms are very special because they
bring together furniture and paintings; which
enables us to discover the major works of *les
Nabis* (Bonnard, Vuillard, and Maurice Denis),
in the settings for which they were created.

Informations

Musée d'Orsay

62 rue de Lille 75343 Paris cedex 07
Tel: 01 40 49 48 14
http://www.musee-orsay.fr
Underground stations: Bac, Solférino or RER C.

Opening hours:

Mondays: closed.
Tuesdays, Wednesdays, Fridays, Saturdays and
Sundays: from 9.30 a.m. to 6 p.m.
Thursdays: from 9.30 a.m. to 9.45 p.m.

Aside from its permanent collections, the
museum offers a wide range of cultural events as
well as educational activities and guided visits.

Lecture visits to the museum collections, to
exhibitions or focused on a single work, for
adults and young people (schools or indivi-
duals), also in sign language; themed days,
courses, lectures, conferences or debates;
audiovisual productions, film cycles, concerts
and performances in the auditorium; works-
hops for children, family visits etc. allowing
all ages of the public to discover the museum
according to their expectations.

A few facts and figures:
Dimensions of the nave:
138 m long
40 m wide
32 m high

12,000 tonnes of metal
framework,
35,000 sq. m. of glazing,
110,000 sq. m. of
timberwork,
944 plasterwork rose
motifs.

Photographic acknowledgements

All illustrations come from Musée d'Orsay documentation, with the following exceptions: Ph. © Photothèque des musées de la ville de Paris - musée Carnavalet, Paris: page 5, 6, 7, 10, 11; Ph. © École nationale supérieure des Beaux-Arts, Paris: 15. Ph. © Michel Guillemot: 48, 49. Ph. © Musée d'Orsay, Dist.RMN-Grand Palais/Sophie Boegly: 50, 51, 53, 54, 55, 56, 57, 59, 60, 61.

Translation: Judith Hayward, Alison Culliford, Charles La Via & Adam Clark-Gimming.

© Nouvelles Éditions Scala 2013
5, rue du Sommerard 75005 Paris France
All rights reserved
ISBN 978-2-35988-099-1
www.editions-scala.fr

Printing: Alpha, Peaugres (Ardèche)
Binding: Façonnage Alain, Féline (Ardèche)
Legal deposit: May 2013